C. C.

21st Century
Skills Library

HEALTH AT RISK

JUNK FOOD

Stephen Currie

Cherry Lake Publishing
Ann Arbor, Michigan

Cherry Lake Publishing

Published in the United States of America by Cherry Lake Publishing
Ann Arbor, Michigan
www.cherrylakepublishing.com

Content Advisor: Carolyn Walker, RN, PhD, Professor, School of Nursing, San Diego State University, San Diego, California

Photo Credits: Cover and page 1, © Don Smetzer/Alamy; page 4, © Cr8tive Images/Shutterstock; page 6, AP Images/Carlos Osorio; page 9, AP Images/Journal Times, Gregory Shaver; page 12, AP Images/Pat Wellenbach; page 14, AP Images/E. Pablo Kosmicki; page 17, Clara Molden/PA Wire; page 19, AP Images/East Valley Tribune, Heidi Huber; page 22, © factoria singular fotographica/Shutterstock; page 24, AP Images/Steve Miller; page 26, © Elke Dennis/Shutterstock; page 28, AP Images/The Indianapolis Star, Rob Goebel

Library of Congress Cataloging-in-Publication Data
Currie, Stephen.
Junk food / Stephen Currie.
   p. cm.—(Health at risk)
Includes index.
ISBN-13: 978-1-60279-284-5
ISBN-10: 1-60279-284-4
1. Junk food—Juvenile literature. I. Title. II. Series.
TX370.C87 2008
641.5973—dc22   2008017498

*Cherry Lake Publishing would like to acknowledge the work of
The Partnership for 21st Century Skills.
Please visit* www.21stcenturyskills.org *for more information.*

TABLE OF CONTENTS

CHAPTER ONE

WHAT IS JUNK FOOD?

While reaching for a stack of chocolate chip cookies may be appealing, cookies will not help you to stay healthy.

You've just gotten home from school, and you're hungry. Time for a snack! Will you reach for apples and carrots? Or will you pick chips, cookies, and cheese puffs?

If you're like most kids in the United States and Canada, you go for the chips and the cookies. Unfortunately, while chips and cookies taste good, they're not so good for you. Foods like these are called junk food. They have unhealthy amounts of fat, sugar, or salt. Junk food can have harmful effects on your body.

You must take in many kinds of **nutrients** to grow, move, work, and play. You get these nutrients from the food you eat and drink. Some nutrients are needed for growth and good health. These

Nutritionists study how foods affect the human body. But nutritionists have many different kinds of jobs. Some nutritionists work in labs. They analyze foods to see what's in them and what they do. Others work for governments. They create programs to improve people's diets.

Still other nutritionists work with people. Some help children and teenagers learn how to eat better. Others help athletes train for their sports. And some work with patients in hospitals. If you become a nutritionist, you'll have lots of possible job choices.

Fast-food French fries may contain trans fatty acids, which contribute to heart problems.

include protein and vitamins. Other nutrients give you energy. These include sugars and fats. The healthiest foods have the right amounts of all these nutrients already in them. Oranges, fish, and beans are good examples.

But not all foods are good for you. Many of the foods you can buy today have too much salt, sugar, or fat. They have much more than your body needs. These are junk foods.

Chips and cookies are two good examples of junk foods. Most cookies are made with butter and eggs, which makes them high in fat. Cookies usually contain plenty of sugar, too. And most cookies don't have enough vitamins or protein to

21st Century Content

Some "junk foods" are unhealthy all by themselves. Others become bad for you when extra salt, grease, or sugar is added. Plain popcorn is not harmful. But popcorn with salt and butter counts as junk food. Another example is chicken. When chicken is baked or roasted, it's usually pretty healthy. When it's fried in oil, though, its fat content shoots up. As a result, most nutritionists call fried chicken a junk food. It's important to look at how a food is made and served before deciding if it's junk.

make up for the fats and sugars. Chips are also high in fat, and of course they have a lot of salt.

You can probably name many other junk foods, too. Doughnuts are high in sugar and fat. French fries are cooked in oil and covered with salt. Bacon is salty and fatty. Candy is full of sugar. These are all called junk food by nutritionists—people who study what's in foods. Junk food is easy to find in stores and restaurants, and maybe in your school and your home too.

CHAPTER TWO

The Popularity of Junk Food

Talesha Gardner, 17, stands in front of soda vending machines in her Racine, Wisconsin, high school. School are starting to remove sugared sodas from school vending machines to help combat childhood obesity.

Junk food may be bad for you—but it's popular. The average American eats over six pounds (2.7 kg) of potato chips each year. In 2005, Canadians spent almost two billion dollars (or about 1.9 billion U.S. dollars) on ice cream. And one survey found that more Americans snack on candy than on fruit or vegetables.

Why do people eat so much junk? One reason is price. Sugar and salt are cheap. Foods that are high in sugar and salt can be sold for very little money. Healthy foods often have more expensive ingredients. So, healthier foods are more costly. Fruit juice, for instance, costs more than cola.

Another reason is convenience. You can eat a bag of cheese puffs months after you buy it. You can't do that with fresh vegetables. Many junk foods are easy to eat when you're on the run, too. You can eat French fries right out of the bag. But you need a fork and a plate to eat a baked potato.

Advertising matters, too. Consumers—people who buy things—often choose to buy products they see in advertisements. In 2005, food companies in the United

States spent about 10 billion dollars (or about 10.2 billion Canadian dollars) advertising junk foods. You can probably name several brands of sugary cereals. But how many brands of bananas can you name?

Some of the biggest advertisers are **fast-food restaurants**. At fast-food restaurants such as Burger King and KFC, much of the menu is high in salt and fat. So, restaurant ads steer people to places that serve lots of junk food.

There's another important reason why junk food is so popular. It tastes good.

21st Century Content

Many junk-food ads are aimed at children. Often, they feature well-known cartoon characters, such as Scooby Doo or SpongeBob SquarePants. Junk food commercials usually have funny scenes and nonstop action, too. Most children enjoy these ads. So, the ads can be very effective in getting children to want these products.

You may be wondering why advertisers would try to target kids. After all, children don't have lots of money, and they can't drive to fast-food restaurants. But Americans 15 and younger spend more money than you might think. They spend billions of dollars each year—much of it on unhealthy snacks advertised on TV. Children also influence what their parents buy. One study found that adults spend 500 billion dollars each year on products that their children ask for. What kind of product do they buy the most? That's right—junk food!

*McDonald's and other fast food restaurants do a good job
of appealing to the popular taste in food—sweet and salty.
Unfortunately, these quick fixes do not promote overall health.*

Most people like the taste of sweet and salty foods. Some experts say that lots of oils and fats really do make foods richer and more flavorful. Others say that we have gotten so used to junk foods that we expect salt or fats in everything we eat. Cost, convenience, and advertising help explain why people eat junk food. But if junk food didn't taste good, no one would eat it! Taste is the biggest reason why junk food is so popular today.

Find an ad for junk food in a newspaper or magazine. Then answer these questions to help you analyze the ad and how it works:

• What does the ad say about the food? Does it mention the taste? Does it mention the price? Does it mention nutrition?

• Are there people in the ad? If so, are they children or adults? What do they look like? What are they doing?

• Does the ad show the food? Does it show the package the food comes in? Why do you think the people who made the ad chose to do it this way?

• Is the ad meant for children or adults? How do you know?

Try it again. This time, use a TV commercial for a different junk food.

CHAPTER THREE

JUNK FOOD AND YOUR HEALTH

In his popular documentary, Super Size Me, *filmmaker Morgan Spurlock went on a McDonald's diet for thirty days to show its harmful effects.*

In 2003, a man named Morgan Spurlock tried an experiment. Spurlock normally ate healthy foods. But for a month he ate all his meals at McDonald's. Though McDonald's sells salads and fruits, most of its menu items are junk foods like bacon cheeseburgers, French fries, and shakes. Spurlock wondered if eating so much junk food would affect his health. It did. In 30 days, Spurlock gained 25 pounds (11 kg). His muscles grew weaker. He started having headaches and chest pains. His doctor told him his liver was damaged. "I was a

Learning & Innovation Skills

Morgan Spurlock is a writer and a filmmaker. He wrote a book and made a movie about his experiment of eating only at McDonald's. Both the movie and the book drew attention to the problems of eating fast food and junk food. Some people say that Spurlock exaggerated some of his problems. Still, the movie was important in making people think about what they eat.

The movie's title comes from the word "supersize," a meal option that McDonald's used for several years. If you "supersized" a meal, you got an extra-large order of French fries and a bigger drink for only a little more money. Critics like Spurlock complained that supersized meal deals tempted people to order calories and salt they didn't need. McDonald's stopped offering supersized meals by 2005. It also added low-fat grilled chicken and fruit to give customers some healthier menu choices.

Junk food has hurt the health of people in countries outside North America, too. One example is the Philippines, a group of islands east of China. In the Philippines, people used to eat mostly rice, vegetables, and small amounts of meat or fish. That was a healthy diet. But in the 1970s, restaurants and grocery stores started selling junk foods. The people of the country began to eat more and more sugar and salt, and fewer vegetables and fish. Once, heart disease and diabetes were rare in the Philippines. Sadly, they are much more common today.

wreck," he wrote later. It took over a year for Spurlock to feel truly healthy again.

Junk food can cause major health problems. Weight gain is one example. Fatty and sugary foods are high in **calories**. Calories are a measure of the energy in food. The more calories, the more you have to exercise to burn that energy. If you don't exercise, your body stores the extra calories as fat—and you gain weight.

Adults usually need 2,000 to 2,500 calories a day. Experts say that even 3,000 calories each day can cause health problems. During his experiment, Spurlock was taking in almost 6,000 every day! Extra calories can lead to

Americans' favored diet of fast food contributes to its reputation as a worldwide leader of obesity.

obesity, or weighing much more than you should. People who are obese cannot move easily. They get tired quickly. The weight strains their hearts and their lungs. They have a much higher risk of heart attack and other serious illness.

Salt causes trouble, too. Eating too much salt can lead to **hypertension**. That means blood is pumped through the body at very high pressure. Hypertension can cause a **stroke**, which may damage the brain. Stroke victims often have trouble moving and speaking.

Diabetes is another disease often related to obesity and poor nutrition. Too much sugar in a person's diet can raise the risk of diabetes. Some people with diabetes lose their eyesight. Others lose the use of their legs. Will these problems happen to you if you eat too many Ring Dings? Maybe, maybe not. But it's best not to try to find out!

CHAPTER FOUR

How Much Is Too Much?

Nutritionist Tim Shields, right, directs Russ Meyers and Gail Meyers on making better food choices while grocery shopping.

Health experts have known for a long time that it's a bad idea to eat mostly junk food. But how much junk food is too much?

It's a good question. But it has no clear answers. Some nutritionists say that since junk food is bad for you, you should never eat it. Morgan Spurlock talked to lots of nutritionists before he began his experiment. Almost half of them said eating junk food was always a bad idea. They saw no reason to put unhealthy food into your body, ever. Junk food, they said, takes up space that should be used for healthy foods.

Some nutritionists also think that junk food is **addictive**. That means that when you eat some, you want more. Your body becomes used to the salts, fats, and sugars. As one health and fitness coach says, junk food "makes you sick, gets you fat and on top of that makes you crave more of it."

Other nutritionists disagree. They don't think junk food is addictive, and they think it's all right to eat a little junk food. "Every once in a while," says a doctor, "it's okay . . . to go out and have ice cream and cake at a party." The risk is especially low for people who get plenty of exercise and eat healthy most of the time.

It's easy to find out if a food is nutritious or if it is junk. You can find information about different foods online and in books. This information is often given in a chart. This example shows part of a chart:

Food	Calories	Total Fat (grams)	Sodium (milligrams)	Protein (grams)
Fruit Yogurt	240	3	140	9
Macaroni and Cheese	250	12	470	5

You can see that the two foods have about the same number of calories. But macaroni and cheese is much higher in fat. It's also much higher in sodium—which means it has much more salt. The yogurt has more protein, which is a good thing. Which is better for you? That's right—the yogurt.

*A young man prepares a healthy fruit salad for lunch.
While such choices take more time in preparation, such
a lunch is far healthier than a candy bar or chips.*

Some experts also point out that it's very hard to stop eating all junk food. Sometimes people say, "I'll never eat junk food again!" But it's hard to keep that promise. "You set yourself up for failure before you start," says one writer. And when you fail, you feel bad—and start eating lots of junk food again. These experts say it's best to try to eat less junk food. That gives you a better chance of keeping your promise—and a better chance of staying healthy.

Suppose you want to cook a meal for dinner tonight. You'll want to choose foods you like. First, choose a main course (such as lasagna, tacos, or stew). Then choose a vegetable, a drink, and a dessert.

It's also important to know about the nutrition in your menu. Go online or find a book with information about nutrition. Look up the foods you chose. Imagine that you eat one serving of each of them. How many calories will you eat at this meal? Try it with a different menu. Does the number of calories change?

CHAPTER FIVE

TAMING THE BEAST

Seventh grader Stephanie Aurora, 12, right, enjoys a salad as classmate Niko Taylor, 13, center, has a cheeseburger and tater tots for lunch at the Nathan Hale School in New Haven, Connecticut. Nathan Hale is part of a district-wide initiative to rid menus of junk food.

All right, so eating candy bars might make you fat. And popcorn loaded with butter can give you hypertension. But junk food is tasty. It's cheap. And it's easy to eat. Junk food is not going to disappear overnight—or maybe ever. So what can we do to "tame the beast" and make sure junk food doesn't cause too many problems?

One plan is to be more aware of the ingredients in the foods you eat. Regular colas use sugar, for instance. But diet colas use a different kind of sweetener that has fewer calories. You can also buy lower-salt corn chips and low-fat cookies. Not all these foods are truly healthy. "Low-salt" foods can be high in calories. "Low-sugar" foods may contain lots of fat. Still, these foods are usually better than the same foods made with regular ingredients.

Some people are using laws to make junk food less dangerous. Many fast-food restaurants use an ingredient called **trans fats**. Trans fats are cheap, so restaurant

*Learning healthy food habits begins at home. Preparing
healthy meals helps develop lifelong habits.*

owners like them. But they can also cause heart attacks. So, some cities are passing new laws to force restaurants to change. New York City, Philadelphia, and Calgary (in Canada) each allow restaurants to use only very small amounts of trans fats.

Education may help, too. Christopher Kimball is a chef who gets people to eat less junk food by teaching them to cook healthy meals. "They try it," he says, "they like it, and they realize what they've been missing." Some groups are running ads to stress the benefits of eating right.

Health education is a basic part of school lessons. So, teachers talk about nutrition and taking care of your body. They remind you to eat healthy foods.

But what does the cafeteria serve for lunch? Many serve greasy cheeseburgers and French fries. And what snacks are in the vending machines? Often, it's candy and potato chips. And look at all those kids buying pop! Schools say to eat healthy—but many make it easy to eat junk.

A group called Parents Against Junk Food wants to change that. This group works for healthier lunches in schools. It wants to ban unhealthy snacks and drinks from school vending machines, too. So far, group members have gotten junk food out of some schools. What junk foods would you be willing to give up? What healthy foods would you like your school to offer?

Martin Mays, 15, stands in line for lunch at his Indiana high school.
This school offers healthy lunch choices instead of junk food.

Junk food can cause problems. But strategies like these can help solve some of those problems. Who knows—maybe you'll come up with a great strategy of your own someday!

Many people in the United States and Canada find it easy to get to a supermarket. But some cities and towns have very few big grocery stores. This can be a problem for people who don't have cars. They often have to buy their food at nearby convenience stores or small groceries instead.

There are two problems with this. One is that these stores charge higher prices. The other has to do with what these stores sell. If you have a convenience store near you, go take a look around. Count how many shelves are crammed with junk foods. Then, count the shelves that have fruit, fresh vegetables, or other healthy foods. Compare it with what you find at a supermarket. What did you discover? Were you surprised?

GLOSSARY

addictive (uh DIK tiv) causing craving, or something you are unable to do without

advertising (AD ver tie zing) telling people about your product

calories (CAL er eez) a measure of the energy in food

consumers (con SOO merz) people who buy things for their own use

diabetes (die uh BEE teez) a disease in which the body can't control sugar in the blood

fast-food restaurants restaurants that have limited menus, low prices, and quick service

fats nutrients found in animal, vegetable, and dairy products such as beef, nuts, and butter

hypertension (high per TEN shun) a disease in which blood is pumped at too high a pressure

ingredients (in GREE dee ents) what a food is made of

nutrients (NEW tree ents) parts of a food that helps people grow and stay healthy

obesity (oh BEE sih tee) weighing much more than is healthy

protein (PRO teen) a nutrient that helps build muscles and organs in the human body

stroke damage to brain cells caused by lack of oxygen, when blood is blocked from getting to the brain

trans fats a type of harmful fat that increases the risk of heart disease

vitamins (VY tih mins) nutrients the body must have to grow and heal

FOR MORE INFORMATION

Books

Cobb, Vicki. *Junk Food.* Brookfield, CT: Millbrook, 2005.

Leedy, Loreen. *The Edible Pyramid: Good Eating Every Day.*
New York: Holiday House, 2007.

Schlosser, Eric. *Chew on This.* New York: Houghton Mifflin, 2008.

Sears, William. *Eat Healthy, Feel Great: A Kid's Guide to Nutrition.*
Boston: Little, Brown, 2002.

Watson, Stephanie. *Fast Food.* New York: Rosen, 2008.

Web Sites

Fast Food Nutrition Facts
www.fastfoodnutrition.org
Information about the nutrients, sugars, fats, and salt in fast-food menus

Kids Health
www.kidshealth.org/kid
Information about eating habits, nutrition, and other health-related food issues

Nutrition Café
http://exhibits.pacsci.org/nutrition
An interactive site with information about nutrition and junk food

INDEX

ABOUT THE AUTHOR

Stephen Currie is a writer and a teacher who is the author of many books. He lives with his family in New York State, where he enjoys kayaking, snowshoeing, and hiking. He is an enthusiastic eater who likes peanut butter, grapefruit, tomatoes, and garbanzo beans and tries not to eat too many chocolate chip muffins.